THOUGHTS HAVE WINGS

*Dedicated to Kerryn
who made my creative life possible.
Also my parents, extended family
and friends, who helped me
in ways only they know.*

My thoughts are like finches in the trees,
if I approach with urgency or intent
they will take sudden flight,
each one a delicate synapse fleeing
into a swirling swarm against the sun,
each one a thought now
beyond my desperate reach.

THOUGHTS HAVE WINGS

JOHN ROSS McGLADE

"To read John McGlade's poetry is to feel the warmth of the clear afternoon light, and be reminded of the fragility and persistence of human life. These poised, lyrical poems have an almost surreptitious intimacy – moments are held tenderly with acute observation and thoughtfulness, "impressions on the edge of knowing". And since McGlade knows that "words have shadows", the book is also peppered with astute aphorisms on the creative process, disarming humour, and some very articulate silences. Thoughts have wings, indeed."
- *Andy Jackson*

"In *Thoughts Have Wings* John McGlade speaks with many voices, each faithful in its moment of experience and reflection and each authentically his. Nourished by beauty, and the need for truth, they are food for the soul."
- *Raimond Gaita*

"What a collection. It is quite extraordinary just how deeply this poetry affects me - I just have to go back, read again and explore the resonance. John Ross McGlade is a master at arranging words in a way that welcomes the reader into his poetry. This collection is a testament from a writer willing to share not only poetry, but also the minutiae that slowly unveils the trajectory of his life. When these pieces are read aloud, they oscillate and the ingenuity of their design becomes apparent."
- *Steve D'Avis*

"John McGlade's poetry burns onto the retina of time, place, and memory. I am drawn into his acute sensitivity to the landscape which, in his poems, becomes a self-portrait of incredible beauty and insight."
- *Wendy Stavrianos*

> "What a peculiar privilege
> has this little agitation of the brain
> which we call 'thought'"
> *David Hume*

The numbered quotes throughout the book
are extracts from
Extemporaneous and Proleptic Thoughts (v.1.),
the journal of John Ross McGlade

Published in 2016
by BIRDFISH BOOKS
birdfish@live.com.au

John Ross McGlade
johnrossmcglade.wordpress.com

Copyright © 2016

All rights reserved. No part of this edition
of this text may be reproduced or transmitted
in any form or by any means, electronic
or mechanical, including photocopy, recording
or any informational storage and retrieval
system, without prior permission from the
publisher.

FRONT COVER
Head of a Youth by Raphael Sanzio

BACK COVER
Three Spikes of No Particular Significance
by John Ross McGlade

Cube on p.5 John Ross McGlade
Chair on p.12 by John Ross McGlade

ISBN-13: 978-0-9953718-0-4

ISBN-10: 0-9953718-0-6

Contents

I Live with These	13
Close to Silence	14
First Flight	15
Home	16
Space	18
Cloud Chamber	18
Escape	19
Traveller	20
Up Late	22
Some Poems	23
The Hammer	24
I Belong in the Rain	27
Fragility	28
Painting Sanity	30
Engines	32
Modulations	34
Completion	36
Drawings of Mice	37
Blue Sea, 1972 - 2013	38
John Matthew McGlade	40
Boolarra Farm 1	42
Catcher on the Road	43
Euclid Burning	44
Before a Poem	45
Certainty	46
Dispositions	48
Drawing 1	50
The Drive	52
Elephants	56
Thoughts from the Farm	58
Birmingham Single	60
Forms	63
Far From Boolarra	64
Moolort Plains	65
Elsewhere	66
The Silence of Books	67
Fitzroy Room	68

Hamish	70
I Wandered Ireland	72
Gestation Blues	73
Hunting	74
In the Beginning	76
Ghosts	77
Icarus	78
Mothers of the Earth	80
Reading	83
Sundays	84
Proust	87
Absence	88
Silence Found Me	89
Solitude Lost	90
Beethoven's Window	91
The Railway	92
Shadows	95
Coleridge's Door	95
What Exists?	96
Poetics and Poetism	100
I do not Reason	101
In the Air	102
The Poet	103
The Painter	103
The Sculptor	104
Thoughts Have Wings	106
Drawing 2	109
Hands	110
Excuse Me, Monsieur	112
Harley Triumph	114
Herbert the Exaggerator	116
First Line Dilemma	117
If Apples fell Sideways	118
Certainties	120
Her Truth	121
For a Girl	122
Hat	124
I Could Not Speak to Her	126
God for Certainty	127

From Schubert	128
Listen	128
Singing in Darkness	129
The Architect	129
The Thickness of Walls	130
All Buildings	131
When we Build in Stone	132
Boollara Farm 2, 1956	134
Rock, Hand, Rain and Air	135
Broken Things	136
Legacies	138
Before	139
Headstone of a Rationalist	140
He Wanted to be Heard	140
Big-noting Myself	140
Writers	141
Poets	141
The Logic of Bathing	142
Old Hands	144
Night Shooting	146
Rage	149
You Read to Me	150
Not There	152
Need	152
Equation	153
Houses without Pianos	153
Anglesea	154
Hills	156
Blackness	157
Leon 4 one 5	158
Going Back	162
Before School	164
Blind	164
Clock	164
Ancestor's Hands	165
Omissions	165
Lost	166
Breathing	168
Oblivion	169

WHY POETRY?

Deciding to publish my poetry was easy because of the people around me. When I began to be aware I was perhaps writing poetry it was never in my mind to publish. I have never aspired to be a poet although I secretly enjoyed some poetry and respected the poet's ability with words. I was often intrigued with the flow of words as they intertwined with meanings, as they do in poetry, however I was suspicious of their power to take over, particularly in the visual arts. Now, upon reflection, I realise there was always a respect for Australian bush poetry in my family and over the years someone would occasionally recite or read a line or two with much pleasure; also I was read poetry in primary school and remembered discovering I was similar to the great poet Wordsworth who lay on his couch and looked with his "inward eye" at daffodils. I realised I was not alone in this tendency and resolved to continue to rejoice in the habit of laying on a couch or sitting under a tree and pondering beautiful things, although there were chores to do. Perhaps Plato was right! However, I was prompted on two fronts to begin to write, the first prompt was a comment from my friend Steve Hope, a fellow artist and blues piano player, who was casually flicking through some of my notebooks when he said "These notes are like poetry", and I noticed a mental jolt within me as he said these words. I had maintained hard-bound note books since my late teens, with puzzling phrases and diagrams as source material for my main practice of fine art, with concerns about systems, perception, my relationships with objects, space and landscape, and of course, creativity. The words in these notebooks would often be isolated on a single page because I didn't want them to be contaminated by other words. Also I was working on the suspicion that by isolation and focus, on these pages, I could consciously mold my subconscious intuitions, but without knowing where I might be led. My second prompt was the death of my uncle years before. In his passing I realised that a lot of his ongoing thoughts and views on life were lost and would only exist in he vague memories of those close to him. With the highly likely event that I would also probably die, I realised I was not leaving my attitudes and inner life to my partner, family and maybe, friends and particularly my children, for them to build on. I don't feel I am narcissistic but this seemed a horrible waste, particularly for 'salt of the earth' fellows like my uncle. I didn't fancy writing in prose and reasoned that the most efficient thing to do was write my inner thoughts down in poetry, no matter how poorly. I said at the time that poetry for me would be talking to myself, honestly, in as few words as possible. Eventually my tentative venture into the public arena was prompted by praise from family and close friends who in their enthusiasm asked when I would publish. Fortunately I live in area of central Victoria that has a lively art community and the streets of Castlemaine are paved with the gold of writers and artists or would be writers and artists. Thanks to poets like Ross Donlan, Ann de Hugard, John Flaus, Steve Davis, Rob Wallis, Tru Dowling, Tegan Gigante, Allis Hamilton, and all the poets of PoetiCas, I was given encouragement to keep on writing; not to leave out the generosity of the venues of the Five Flags Hotel and the Food Garden Café in central Castlemaine. In my case, this is 'Why Poetry' – plus the sheer pleasure of it!

Note: Some of the poems in this collection are available as real time writing videos, with music, on my blog:
johnrossmcglade.wordpress.com

CR

> **1. Poetry is talking to myself, honestly,**
> in as few words as possible.

CR

I Live with These

At the center of an empty room
with a wooden floor
there is a simple wooden chair.
The room is slightly worn
and has plaster walls.

The chair, not new,
is facing away from me.
The light is dim;
the room is lit from
one direction,
coming from the wall
facing the chair.
The light is natural
by day,
artificial at night.

It is of soft intensity
casting a soft shadow
on the floor.
A discovery
I keep returning to,
a room to be explained,
a chair held in a room.

I live with these thoughts,
a complexity of simple things
and they are
my bliss,
they are
the pleasure of my consciousness.

Close to Silence

Whenever she drew
she was close
to the silence of things.

In the hard shadows
she saw the light
across soft breasts.
By the charcoal's mark
she followed the milk skin
of silent women
still, for her.
In their mute beauty,
quiet as flowers.

Often she drew
at night
where the edges
of the paper disappeared
into her room.
By the soft light
of kerosene,
she made her marks
close to the silence
of her own beauty,
to be drawn
across her own page
into the silence
of her eyes.

ଓ

> **678. I suspect** the best way to articulate what a visual artwork is about is in poetry.

First Flight
for the love of gliding over hills and plains

I felt the hand of God
in the wind of the hill;
from the rain
of that paddock
I was lifted.

As I ran
down the green
beautiful grass,
that rippled
with a power unseen,
that straddled my belly,
lifting me gently into
Lilienthal's dream.

Like a child held high
the first time
by my father's big hand
in a room
while my mother watched.
I was there again,
taken by the soaring
of my soul.
On that day
I flew,
not to a ceiling
but to the sky
of my life.

Home

I grip at the earth,
for a while now,
the soil tight in my hand.
This dirt from another time,
when I played in the grasses
down by the creek
that passes Boolarra,
of tree-ferns and moss
green over black rocks
where the speckled trout hid below,
and my brother Robert,
as we called him then, and I
caught them on safety pins
with just brown string for the line.

In those days
it was full,
and you could hear it
like the voices of the old people
as you came down the track;
but, I would wager,
not now.

The moist mud-black dirt
was putty in my hands,
and the beat
of the milking machine
in the evening
echoed down the valley
to Bailie's farm
and, I suspect, beyond.

As the last cows
were turned out
by Uncle George,
with steam from nostrils
they sunk in the mud,
and we turned for the hill
and home.

ஐ

> **672. Some poems** of mine
> are to be understood by me
> at a later date.

Space

I need the space of no interruptions
to think into the long hours of the night.
Into the pleasures of conscious thought
born in the lonely paddocks
and vacant times,
vacant days,
precious days when I dreamed
in the soft grasses of time.

ଔ

> **676. Good poets** can be accurate
> about the things we have difficulty in being
> accurate about.

ଔ

Cloud Chamber

Perhaps
we are just
the vapor trails
left by the particles
of our souls
in a chamber
of existence.

Escape

I escape into
the words of my night.
They do not let me down.
They are wise
as they descend from my pen
and explain many things
I was not aware
I had been carrying
in my soul.

༺ ༻

1840. Proleptic Poetry.
(Proleptic: spontaneous thought provoked by
sense perception alone without reflection).
This is how I write many poems. I begin with
perhaps a line or phrase that I notice intrigues
me, then I respond to these words on the page to
generate the next line spontaneously without
much thought. The subject or object of the poem
will evolve as the lines accumulate.
I suspect that, in our educated culture,
we tend to think we must have an idea for art
before we begin.

Traveller

I come from a time
when we looked out of windows
to people moving
and wildebeest stampeding,
when no human or beast was there.
I come from a time
where words and songs
came from things in empty spaces
where no-one was speaking
and no-one was singing
but there were suns
in every room.

I have lived through the times
where words and people
from war-torn lives
of hunger and despair
passed through our bodies
with a ghostly ease
that no-one feels or even cares,
and there were machines,
without a man or woman,
suspended in the air,
made from oil and stones,
travelling to kill families
seeking refuge
in buildings from the earth.

And I will tell of my time
where I said gentle words
to loved ones I could not see
in places far,
through melted rocks and sands
as fine as human hair
and reflections from machines
not in this world.

In those days
I lived alone
amongst millions of beings
who wrote on machines
with small lightning
you could hold in your hand.
Oh how I wish we could travel now
and be with me there.

☙

1684. The act of writing changes thought.

Up Late

As I sit at my desk
in the night
of my sanctuary
there is the silence I know
from a time before I had words,
and now it returns
as it always returns
while others sleep
in the silence of their dreams.
I breathe
slow thoughts
of many things
lost to the day
of rabble and reason.
I am at peace with my mind.
I enjoy its company
and we make our old pact
long before we had words,
to be in the darkness
and wish for the rain.

ଔ

1564. Poetry is not just for information;
it's also for impressions on the edge of knowing.

Some Poems

Some poems
I prefer to read in the night
by a fire, when my mind
and the world
are still.

Some poems are for the night
but require the sound
of rain on the roof.

Some are for a quiet window
to a green paddock
that sweeps up to the trees
of a childhood past.

Others I prefer to read
in an empty room
with no windows
at the top of wooden stairs
in Fitzroy.

Some poems are for the grave,
to be read in the wind
when a poet dies.

And some are for
the dreams of the living,
needing revelations
for the solitudes
of their souls.

The Hammer
for Julien, my son

As I sit at my desk
with my pen scratching
I hear my son hammering outside
as I used to do.

I have no hammer now,
only words
to write through the world of ideas,
to nail thoughts
to the mast of pages.

My son builds
with the dignity of labour,
with an authenticity
that I hope for
in the tricks of words.
He is in a physical world
with hand and mind united,
in an intelligence
I once knew.

Like father, like son
and my father before,
he has no need to stop
this delight in matter,
in a pleasure of craft
with mind.
No need to discount
a respect for the wisdom
of the hands
as some with pens do.

His hands,
once smooth and small,
are now thicker than my
worn things,
and have the strength
of the timbers
he fashions.

The lines of labour
will furrow deep
into his psyche.
He will weave his story
with timber, metal
and machines.
Through the scribe
of his trades,
written in the structure
of the things he has made.

No doubt
his hand clasps the hammer
with the certainty
beyond the hand
that holds my pen.
My hand builds tentatively
in the fragility of words,
with the silent construction
of thoughts
forming across a page.

From a software of memories,
perceptions,

and calculations.
Drawn up
from the abstract wells
of ephemeral intuitions
and reason.

My thoughts return
to my desk, the room,
where books are my tools.
With the objects I need to think,
and images of things made
by my own effort
from a time before,
when I was like him.

And I?
I am content.
I am left with
the bliss of ideas
on the edge of my knowing,
and the comforts of poetry
and love
that will eventually
allay the softness
of these hands.

And, although I work
without the sound of a hammer
affirming my existence
echoing from the hills,
I live in the vanity of hope
that some of my words
will echo in the hearts of others.

I Belong in the Rain

I belong in the rain.
It is my home.
First, in Gippsland hills.
Wet bracken
to my soul.

In lanes of any city
I am home
as it rains,
quietly not foreign
anymore.

In narrow doorways,
waiting to cross
the familiar
wet black
that shines
traffic lights
under my boots,
I am home again
in the Gippsland hills
on the Boulevard St Germain.

 катка

1177. When I write poetry or paint, I am.

Fragility

'We are blind with compasses
in our hands'
— W. S. Merwin

I too easily
forget the fragility
of sacred things.
I forget the fragility
of my normality.
In the comfortable rooms
of my possessions,
my distractions forego
my being.

In ignoring
the fragility
of a hard-won democracy,
I am blind to the fragility
of the words
of my ancestors
that keep me free.

I am the thief, the robber
on the roads
to reason with compassion.
I attack with the knives
of ignorance and suspicion,
killing those
that think
or flee.

I am the individuated one
in the mob
that knows my rights,
complicit in a slow demise
of my obligations.
I am the one that
seeks and marks borders
against our common humanity.

In laziness and opulence
I sit before electric screens,
preferring the shallows
of mediocrity,
and lose the fragility
of my soul.

I forget the necessity for tolerance
except for my own kind
and avoid morality,
as I defer to the secure,
absurd logic
and the self-righteous stealth
of our expanding bureaucracies.
Abdicating thinking,
I pretend all is well.

Painting Sanity

At the edge of his vision,
in the penumbra of his thoughts,
not in the distinct shadows
of certainties,
he leaves colours
across the canvas
of his ephemeral days.

In abstractions
too far,
many are lost,
straying from
the real
in the vanities
of novelty,
for novelty's sake.

In the preference
for doubt
he has security
not knowing
where his images
will lead,
where anything leads.

There were times when
all was reasoned,
all was planned,
excluding the passions
of a child

across fields
of long grasses,
that rippled
in the wind,
that swayed
in the wind
where he played.

But now he rests
in the logic of uncertainty,
comfortable, for now,
when every stroke,
every gesture,
every word
a puzzle

worth pursuing
like the grasses
in the wind
to the edge
of his vision.
To the shadow's edge
of his thoughts,
where his sanity
now lies.

༄

> **85. All my life I have been wary of words.**
> They are not the full story.

Engines
with thanks to my parents

I remember engines hidden.
One, in the still white
of a foggy morning
as I lay in warm,
with protestant guilt,
it thumped, thumped, thumped out
over the damp hills north of Mirboo,
beckoning me to milking machines,
radio news, and Jersey milk
through the separator,
filling galvanized cans
that would proudly stand,
later, down on the road.

In the sun
I remember another,
with the singing moan
of a long-ago saw
like the black crows' call.
And the smell of the dust,
from green hardwood,
floating in shafts of sunlight
through holes in iron,
stinging my eyes.

As the flat belt
flew long and over
the green flywheel,
spinning, spinning,

the whole shed shook
on a floor of dust and chips
from the axe and saw,
milled from the bush
just up there.

And in the evening,
a single-shot motor,
muffled, bangs
in the distance,
ignition timed
by the logic
of spinning weights
with no rhythm,
down in the scrub,
away from the house,
pumping alone.

I remember these,
with magnetos
and governors
with fondness and wonder,
and pistons and valves,
their glorious rhythms
that pumped into the heart
of my childhood's dreaming.

଼

> **2131. What is left out** of a poem
> is just as important as what has been put in.

Modulations
in respect of Tesla

We are the ones that talk
silently through the walls
of your rooms,
over your mountains
to infinity.
You don't know or hear
our words
as we pass through
your matter,
your breathing.
At every breath
we are there,
when you sleep
with our thoughts
under your beds,
our words
through your dreams
everywhere,
all your life.
We, the silent wanderers
with ideas
in every tree,
every flower,
every bird,
every tear.
Our words are there
unwritten
in sounds unheard.

We are images
you cannot see
by the light
through your eyes.
You are blind,
existing in all
our colours,
you are unaware
we are there,
passing through the ones
who have mastered
what you don't understand.
We are the ones
in the waves
of the universe
that have made ourselves
unheard, not seen.

☙

> **22. I can use poetry** to describe or speculate, but I prefer to use it to discover what my mind is thinking, unannounced to me. Through actions I discover/create myself.

Completion

In the silence
of his separation,
still seeking remoteness,
he invites his muse
to bring the poetry
of simple words.

In the mix of things
he knows very little
before he begins.
Drawing from within
the muse that may come,
as he sits and begins
in the room
of his stories,
an artist
of the invisible.

On the blank pages
of desire, that affirm
his connection
to the solitude of living,
in his receptivity
to this abyss,
the ritual of writing
will complete the silence
of his separation,
and in the rhythm
of the pen
the words
of the night
will come.

Drawings of Mice

I am brought back
to the old house
by a poem
and the sound of rain
outside my window
that settles in
for the day.
Like many days,
long ago,
they comfort me
with a love from
the kitchen
I know is there
by the old combustion stove
and the green enamel
cast-iron sink,
and my mother's drawings
in Indian ink,
of cartoon mice
in a side drawer.
Standing on my toes
staring in,
playing across a page
amongst strings and things,
now lost forever
from a young girl's dreams
to the scurry
in the wheel
of life and things,
put aside
for later.

Blue Sea, 1972 - 2013
*thoughts outside the "Blue Sea"
in Castlemaine*

There is a discrepancy
between the feeling
of now in place
and the feeling
of before
that comes over me
as a strange sadness,
a shifting phase,
when in a familiar place
I have known
for many years,
every day,
now lost at sea.

Now, I do not know
as I did.
Now, I do not feel
as I did,
in that past time
although all of now is
the same.

It is different perhaps
in a memory regained.
In a passing wave to
how I felt then,
to how, in familiarity,
I feel now.

An existential slippage,
outside on the footpath
after buying chips,
of place and time.

Between my words
and thoughts
out of register,
in an experiential overlay,
there is a discrete shift
into a sadness
of things lost.

I do not know
what this difference is,
but sometimes that difference
is why I do not return
to places I know.

○○

> **2123. Good art and good poetry
> oscillates** in the mind
> between the discernable and the indistinguishable.
> This oscillation gives pleasure
> throughout the mind and with the body.

John Matthew McGlade
1884 – 1943. V81537

An Irishman,
a Belfast gentleman,
he was gone
before I was born
to his daughter
who later gave his first name to me.

She was told a cruel thing:
don't cry,
think of your brother –
Jack has lost his father.
She was only thirteen.

Before, he was shot in a Great War,
more than once,
at Gallipoli.
In Egypt his horse
was shot beneath him
in the bloody heat and sand.

But he just wrote letters,
without a fuss,
as if all was ordinary.
Except the flies
on the bodies.

Give my regards
to all at Glen Sheira,
Bill and his brother
are in the same troop as me.
I may be home by Christmas.

She waited,
long.
He came, eventually,
home.
And married her
and farmed those hills,
despite Gallipoli.

But I never met him
on those steep paddocks
of my home, of Gippsland,
amongst the cows he milked,
the yards he cleaned.

She remembered later
her dad said *Poodlebury*
instead of Puddlebury
in the long bush nights
of Combinebar,
reading to his children.

He was a Prefect
and James Joyce, as a boy,
whispered
watch out for McGlade
along the corridors
of Clongowes Wood.

And I was with him,
along those corridors,
in a portrait
of an artist
who walked in trepidation,
down a passage to a door
before I was born.

Boolarra Farm 1

Before I knew words
I remember many things,
on the road unsealed
that wound
up the tree-fern valleys,
through the stringy-bark
straight and tall
to the land of my beginning.

Cut into the hills
along one side
to the place where
the gully met,
then along the other side,
again and again.

By rounding hills,
by crossing gullies
into a dream,
that is my home.
A land of wandering days,
with no one.

ଔ

> **1632. The purpose of my writing**
> is to really get inside my experience,
> not further away.

Catcher on the Road

It was made by my father
with his care
and delight
of doing a job well.
In ply and clear lacquer
a case that unfolds
with all he needs
in the nineteen-fifties,
for them,
screaming in the night
on tar and bloody gravel
behind a tow truck,
perhaps at Picnic Point
on the Princess,
a limb in the grass,
a baby to be christened
before dying.
V. L. 3 T. L.
Come in please.
Three kids at home,
Kath by the phone
and Bluey to his friends.
With respect and reason
he made it
with compartments
for different things,
pragmatic divisions
with care, for sanity,
for a job well done.

Euclid Burning
*a response to an imposed logic
on an old continent*

Perhaps on entering
the world
too fast
something was lost,
not noticed
about this land.

Worn by our
incessant logic
imposed
in the diagrams
of angles,
we have calculated
and neglected
the rocks with hands
from the ones
here before.

They were with the earth
lacking the geometry
of our Hellenic past,
or so it seemed to us.

But now, in the fires
of Euclid burning,
though things are lost
our memories are not.
And we perhaps belong
or so it seems
on this land of dreams,
this continent of fire.

Before a Poem

Before a poem
there is a dwelling
in the mind.
While my pen
is suspended
over the page
there is a settling
in thoughts
not yet formed.
A settling through
my body, felt.
A settling of a knowing
yet to be.
A settling in a dwelling
only resolved by a pen,
leaving words
like paint
across a canvas.
A settling on the page
in time
that I only begin
to understand.

ca

> 1402. I write poetry to discover.

Certainty

Certainty is a poison
that distorts
the truth.

Or…

The poison
of certainty
kills
the truth.

Or…

The man
who is certain
is far from
the truth.

Or…

Certainty
that God is
on their side
is the mark
of fools.

Or…

Certainty is a poison
that distorts
the growth
of the truth.

Or ...

Certainty
has many things
to answer for.

Or...

If one is really
certain
one is most likely
wrong.

༂

---

270. Art and poetry
are not meant to make things more obscure
but to make them more known.
This does not mean art is accessible
to the lazy mind. Effort must be undertaken.
For art, you may need to change your mind.

Dispositions

What will the morning
light give, modulated
by the trees?

What words will,
what writer give,
what unintended thought
will come to me?

What will someone say,
that I notice, I notice
to keep for later,
for finding casually?

What will I put together,
that was not together before?
What thing or event
will align with words
for the pleasure of my mind?

What secret will be in eyes that meet,
that cross a room,
with the passing of a cloud?

What music or poetries of thought
will raise me to a higher place?
Succinctly, giving
where they have never given before.

What lines will I draw
from my dispositions,
what words will escape my pen?
What colours will move across a surface
to pleasurable unknown ends?

What things will I arrange
on what I have seen
fleetingly
beneath my hands?

What would I have said of my life,
when loved ones are gone,
if none of these passions
had come to pass?

༄

2328. When I begin a poem
it is usually with noticing my delight in a phrase
I have heard, that plays on my mind and is like music
to my ears. Then I write the phrase down or type it,
and the mere of writing begets the next line
and so on; after this process of writing lines
that lead to more lines,
I discover an insight into myself that I was unaware of
until the poem was completed; this is the wisdom that
creating poetry gives from the pleasure of hearing.

Drawing 1

From the soft light
of my morning study
I hear the silence
of my daughter drawing.

As I am drawn back
from my thoughts,
I know the pleasure
she has found
in the quiet unity
of paper, pen, and mind.

No longer the excitement
of the sun as a circle
with radiating lines,
for the bliss of a child
discovering her power
in abstract signs
over a reality
as it is forming.

No longer the lost wandering
of teenage years
with retail distractions,
television taunts, timetables,
avoiding P.E.
and the long uniformity
of dress codes.

There is now,
from another room,
the silence of acceptance,
of the validity
in the world of adults.
That the hand that reveals
its path across a surface
is a window into the world
of the intellect,
silently
balanced with the soul
by a line
she will draw
through her life.

ଔ

> **1179. When I write poetry or paint** there is a certain amount of conscious decision-making but mainly a lot of being directed by subconscious intuitions.
> Balancing these two types of thought is the skill.

The Drive

My brother rang
and left a message
to ring him back,
when I can,
he has some sad news.

I had to return,
against my better judgment,
to the new roads bypassing
my childhood.
We went down,
as my partner drove,
back in time
onto new asphalt ribbons
of speed in comfort,
of new signs
to places I once knew,
but not now,
all but obliterated
in the efficiency
of public works
and the rationality
of engineers
throwing poetry aside.

Nar Nar Goon, Robin Hood, Officer,
Bunyip and Boolarra, resonated
but were now just
big green signs
to nowhere.
Diversions not taken
at one hundred and ten K's.

With no time, not now,
for little places.

Down into the sad valley
we went, the valley
of coal, smoke stacks and grazing cows,
and huge digging machines
positioned, for off ramp views,
by proud citizens
of the past.

Eventually we found
the small roads
I remembered
and the village
I had lost.

In front of the church
I saw the hearse
about to leave,
people milling around
and bright flowers
for Georgie, my aunt;
we were late,
myself, by years.

At the reception,
in a new kindergarten hall,
behind my mother's old school,
I was kissed by many women
who were old like me,
amongst too many sandwiches and cakes
the ladies of the day had organized.

And I shook hands with cousins
spruced up in new suits and ties.
With the hands of their fathers and fathers before
that were now theirs.
Hands, that I remembered
I respected for their honesty,
thick and gnarled and proud,
like old trees
with lines of ingrained work,
not like my soft things
that only presses keys.
And their children and grand children
one by one, beautiful adults,
beautiful offspring.

There was Hugh and Mack Stagg there too!
Echoes of my mother's genes.
Hugh, whose voice broke late,
ambled across the car park
and I stretched out my arm
to greet the old bugger,
so pleased to see him!!
I remembered Mack's face,
quiet, with deep-set eyes
and a Samuel Beckett stare.
A fine horseman of the high country,
(as all the brothers were)
still lean as a string bean
like Georgie's Jack
(an anathema to the Stagg clan).

He always slept on the veranda when home
and later my brother told me
he has seen, years ago, an iconic scene
of Mack on his horse,
going hell for leather, standing in stirrups
with stock-whip cracking over head,
that stays clear in his mind to this day.

On a screen set up
there was a video playing
(with my sister singing,
and occasionally, bagpipes)
of pastel colour photos from Georgina's life
of marriages, babies, graduations, flowers
and, of course, beloved cactus and the farm.

My partner commented,
while driving back,
that Georgina was quite beautiful
when she married Jack!
She could see why he fell for her.
The general consensus
was whispered in my ear,
by Jackie, my cousin's wife,
that at 96 she had a good innings
and I was not about to argue with that!
And I thought to myself,
the drive was worth it, tenfold
and more.

Elephants

I wont go out today,
there's an elephant in my room
somewhere.
Besides, it's windy.

I will stay in
and look for it.
They are usually in the corners,
but I've checked,
it's not there.

I suspect it's African,
with big ears,
so it will hear me.
In my experience,
you can't surprise them.

If it's Irish,
I will never find it.
They are very small
and clever,
and they know my mind.

I will just sit still,
and think nothing.
That usually flushes them out.
They may eventually move
under these circumstances.

My room is partly furnished
by classical assumptions,
handed down from my family.
Some are from my friends, or books.
They can cower behind them,
but they can also, inadvertently,
reveal a tail or two.

I have one borrowed chair
(from a skip)
in philosophy.
But, if I'm sitting on it,
I Kant see behind me!
So no luck there.

Windows are useful.
If the sun is in a reasonable position
and the glass is clean,
there may be enough light
to see an elephantine outline,
even in the shadows.

As I said, it is windy,
and there is little sun today
so I will just lie
on my bed of comforts
and hope he goes away.

Thoughts from the Farm

I wonder about cows,
then dogs,
then sheep and horses,
less about chooks.
Cows stand in paddocks all day
and all night.
Do they think?
To what extent
do they examine their lives?
Or do they examine it
in ways we don't know?
Socrates would have a field
(or paddock) day.

Are their lives worth it to them?
What are their assumptions?
If they are just on automatic pilot
what is God doing?
What are cows doing and why?
Why are they here on this planet?

I think I would be bored being a cow.
They spend most of their time just eating.
Then again, they can relieve themselves
right there,
without going to a special room,
when they feel like it,
and other cows don't seem to mind.
What's going on?

I also wonder about artists,
in fact I envy them.
They just seem to do it,
as if it is ordinary for them.
They stand or sit in their studios,
or looking out windows,
sometimes all day and night,
without questioning why they should,
which philosophers sometimes do,
which is at least commendable.

But artists just seem like cows,
on automatic pilot,
chewing the cud again and again,
regurgitating the esoteric.
Oh! They may ask questions,
but not why they should do it
in the first place.
What's going on?
If God exists, what trick is it playing?
Even with the chooks, looking at me.

ɞ

> **1121. Poetry is not an attempt to obscure**
> reality, but to get closer to it.

Birmingham Single
for my children

BSA ridged frame
1939, 500cc. side valve.
My first single ever.
Over Shepparton channel-country humps
it thumped out a song of a machine
against a father's words,
into the warm night of oblivion
from cash in hand
and a deal done sweet.

Lawrence of Australia
through the back blocks
of the flat, sleeping land
of my adolescence
in the seventies,
into the long streets
of suburban banalities
in country towns.

Under old tyres
bitumen blurred
narrow to the pampas grass,
straight as a die,
watching as we cleaved the wind
with the deep throb of pleasure,
of an iron-cast affirmation.
Through the hot blued-chrome trumpet
she sang a rhythm
for my heart,
as plovers took flight.

That night
I soared in the sparks
of nihilism defeated,
igniting a freedom found,
an existential bliss held tight
in the gauntlets
of ancient knights
across the vast lands
of suppressed lust,
down to the beautiful music
of a single piston firing
in a cylinder of dreams.

With the twist of a hand
I was dragged into the ecstasy
of speed,
as she pulled away
forward into the darkness
with the smell of hot oil
reticulating,
that sublime intoxicant
of machines
that I knew.

Dropping down
through the gears
she held me,
pushed me down
into the black leather

to accelerate
away again
to the wild edge
of reason.

Birmingham Small Arms
held me
as I sang the holy praise
of all machines
with the moon,
the dreamings
and the wind;
in the machinations
of our first time
into the bliss
of that night
she seduced innocence
into forever.

BSA M20 1939. 500cc single cylinder motorcycle (Never sell).

419. Meaning comes through doing.

__F'r B'dls__

APPEAR TO GIVE IT WHAT IT WANTS
AS QUICKLY, SUCCINTLY
AS POSSIBLE
YOU HAVEN'T GOT TIME
TO WASTE
TO LET IT KEEP NIPPING
AT YOUR HEELS
LIKE A FEARFUL PUP
YOU HAVE MORE IMPORTANT
THINGS TO DO
LIKE BEING IN LIFE
BEING HUMAN OR DOING NOTHING
JUST DON'T LIE TO YOURSELF
AS YOU FILL IN FORM AND BE
POLITE. THEY, IN THEIR BLINDNESS
WILL BE HAPPY TO TICK A BOX
THAT IS ALL THEY NEED

Far from Boolarra

I have found another home
in Paris,
far from Boolarra
on my returns
to the rues and boulevards
and the long narrow nights
in the rain of my silent wanderings.

I have ruminated
at every step
on wet stones.
Over the gutters of the sweepers
with curved witches' brooms,
where thought is respected.

I feel succinct
in small rooms
conducive to writing.
The stairs the same
as they were before.

And before
my country wrote,
they were here.
History was recorded
in the steps of poets,
in the wear of timbers,
and with the smoothing of stones,
worn by persistence of ideas.
They too belonged
to the rain of Paris,
as I do,
once more.

Moolort Plains

The rhythms of my life
follow the flow of this land
from the horizon's curved line
to the granite's proud stance,
from old posts grey with rust wires
run through into the beginning
of my soul.

As rippling grasses race away,
revealing the sinews of the wind,
they imbue the lines drawn
across my heart, that sing
with the songs of this earth.

I too, suffer.
I too, know its beauty,
its fragility to the avarice of men,
who hide behind shallow reason
complicit with the law
that dances in a blindness
of justice for the few.

In the quiet nights, as I stand
looking out across thoughts
wrought in my day,
it modulates them
with a stillness, a solitude
of sacred rhythms,
of a land set deep
into the tempo of my living,
set deep in humanity's soul.
And I worry such things
will be lost to the winds.

Elsewhere

Some day,
words will appear
in the air
and our days will come
to a time
when nothing
is there
and the wind
will be no more.

The trees will have spoken
of happier times,
their leaves
no longer here.
The birds will have
gone to the sun
and our souls,
on another horizon,
will eventually be free.

ଔ

> **1774. My thoughts are like pigeons**
> in the square, if I approach them with urgency
> and intent, they quickly fly away.

The Silence of Books

I wander in the silence of books,
through the architecture of shadows
in the mind.
The music of cathedrals is gone
to the quiet of the stars
and humanity
no longer sings
to the earth
the ancient songs
of the sea and the sky.

☙

> **687. As a poet all I need** is one line.
> As a painter all I need is one mark
> and as a maker all I need is the metal in my hand.

Fitzroy Room
from the sound cube system, 1972

In that room
with no windows
my machine
was running.
It listened
to my breathing
and gave it back
to upstairs.
On a hot quiet Sunday
when I was drawing,
and the scratching
across paper
came back to me
with my breathing.
At first from one wall,
then the others.
From the ceiling
and the floor.
Creating a distance,
beyond this place.
A space extending
as my footsteps
went into the walls.

In the laneway down below
a distant dog
barked and came to me
with the sounds of breathing,
with the sounds of my lines drawing,
up the stairs
onto a landing
outside my door.

And in each rotation
in six directions.
Wall by four,
ceiling, floor,
over and around
a canine crying
through the walls,
around and around
away and away,
layer with layer,
with a drawing,
with a breathing
lost in sounds,
a music distorted
of their making,
from a room,
blending, modulating, breathing
into a darkness receding
from this time,
from this room,
to infinity.

ଓ

> **1214. I write poetry** to extend my thinking.

Hamish
for Hamish

Listening to children
I sat amongst their parents
and I was proud,
like they were,
of their confident offspring,
who spoke in their young ways
at their graduation,
from that small red-brick school
in that small country town.

My son stood
in front of the microphone,
as I no longer can,
saying he wanted to be an architect
or a stand up comedian
and everybody laughed with him.

I thought again,
he's got the gift of the gab
and a bit of the 'divel' in him,
as my mother would say.

Since small
he had a way about him!
A way with words
that endeared him to me
through quizzical thoughts
and innocence.
I told him stories,
I loved him.
I loved his mind.

Now, without speech,
perhaps I rely on him
to continue his Irish tradition
from his great-grandfather
to my mother down.
He can tell stories,
caught up in the tale,
unprompted and lively
with an unrealised love of words,
wit, and the music of speaking.
One night at my desk
I heard him on the radio.
With authority
he held banter
like I used to do.

I recalled my embarrassment
when at ten
my primary school headmaster
burst into our chalk dust room
declaring I had the voice for radio
and a likely career
to all and sundry.

Now, I listen to children
and think of my son,
in the familiar sounds
of inner thoughts,
that perhaps some day
he too will have his children
listening to the music of words
from him.

I Wandered Ireland
walking in 1980

I wandered Ireland alone,
over the graves
down the streets
along the lanes
of green and stones

to my past,
land of songs,
voices of my families
deceased
I did not know,

into the rains of my home.
I am their dream,
a continuous line,
drawn to me
through histories
and their miseries,

from joys, long forgotten.
I hear them asking,
in a church yard
of green and stones
beneath the trees'
dark canopies,

amongst the moss
of yesterdays,
from their shadows
here now,
where are your children?
What are your dreams?

Gestation Blues

I admitted to my lover
my weakness and indiscretion.
I had again betrayed her
by sleeping with another.
Yes! I had gone to bed
with a very attractive thought
that came to me out of the blue
while I was at the pub,
and seduced me with its beauty.

This thought kept me up
until the early hours
with its narcissistic demands.
It wanted satisfaction,
so I stripped it back
to its bare essentials,
then proceeded from there
to play with it
in all the ways I could imagine.

It was a good-time thought
and had left before I woke.
I felt a loss, cheated.
I vowed never to take
just any floozy thought
home again.

Nine months later
I was standing on my doorstep
and out of the blue
a poem arrived.

Hunting

I hunt for words
not yet spoken
to make clear
things unknown
until I say them
without reason
then some are clear,
some are known.

I hunt for objects
not yet existing
to make clear
things unknown,
until I make them
without reason
then some things come clear,
some things known.

I hunt for images
not yet seen
to make clear
things unknown,
until I draw them
without reason
then some things are clear,
some things known.

I hunt for notions
not yet thought,
to make clear
thoughts unknown,
until I think them
without reason,
some things clear
some unknown.

ॐ

> **199. Artists and poets are travelling blind,**
> like the rest of humanity,
> but occasionally they take a glimpse
> and do something about it.

In the Beginning

In the silence
of his separation,
still seeking remoteness,
he invites his muse
to bring the poetry
of simple words.

In the mix of things
he knows very little
before he begins.
Drawing from within
the muse that may come,
as he sits and begins
in the room of his stories,
an artist of the invisible.

On the blank pages of desire
that affirm his connection
to the solitude of living,
in his receptivity
to this abyss,
the ritual of writing
will complete the silence
of his separation,
and in the rhythm of the pen
the words of the night will come.

ca

> **164. Words have shadows.**

Ghosts

As we step from the page of our life
there are the ghosts of words unwritten
for the ghosts of thoughts unsaid.
The ghosts of things not promised
to the ghosts of lovers ended,
or the ghosts of friends departed,
with the ghosts of those before
and the ghosts of the dead.

There are the ghosts of music not played.
For the ghosts of songs unsung
and the ghosts in empty beds
in the ghosts of our lost rooms.

There are the ghosts in the walls
in the houses of our memories
with the ghosts of closed doors
that know the ghosts of open windows
out which our dreams flew.
To the ghosts of the rain,
the ghosts in our tears,
as we step from the page
there are the ghosts of our decisions
never made
through the ghosts of our fears.

༄

> **301. Words are not true,**
> they are just advantageous.
> The words of the poet can be closer to the truth.

Icarus

I have walked on the air
of times long past.
I have walked with the breeze
of the mountain pass
that lifted my wing
of aluminum and wire
to fly with the eagles
there.

Beneath the clouds, high
above the long plains
of human despair,
above the ploughed paddocks
of raw heat and earth,
Icarus and I fly now
on the heat of his sun
beyond the ancient legend
of his demise.

No wing of wax
to melt by the sun,
no father crying
'come back, son'.
We soar, merged
into a bliss,
as one.

Our souls united high
on an Icarus dream
we soar
in the domain of eagles
on the thinnest of air,
at one with the mighty
there.

At one with the scribes
of the legends of men,
who dreamed of flight
when bound to the ground,
of a freedom yearned
in times long passed,
of a freedom
to walk on the air.

Of a freedom
in the bliss of a dream,
not to be slain
by the doubts of men,
not to be slain
by the sun again.

ೞ

> **1062. What use is a poet?**
> What use is our soul with no voice?

Mothers of the Earth
for Wendy, from 'Field number 3'

I am in a vast field
on a vast canvas,
serenity on a wall,
with a lone stooped woman
in peasant dress.
Isolated, in a small square halo.
A frame of emphasis,
a painters choice
of golden hues,
of the grasses
from a time
before her own.

I feel her painter's
still reverence for her.
For all women
by patience who toiled.
Of meticulous hours
as she too works,
stooped,
framed in a studio
over her field of colors.
She is the same,
she is with her.

There has been always
a load to bear
for women.
The fallen twig kindling
for the fire that gives warmth,
is gathered in the woods
of her heritage,

in the wisdom
of the artist's years.
She feels for them,
as I do now.

Of reasons to feed
their children
from the paddocks of Ireland,
she now thinks in paint
to explain the dignity
of her sisters,
her mothers
gone.

I can sense the earth
and heat of the crop.
The earth in the clothes.
The earth in their breathing.
The earth in their souls.

There is a dignity
in a quiet servitude
with aprons and scarves
without men.
They know
the forces of nature
that all women carry,
at one with the earth.

A raw elegance exists
in paint over a surface,
a texture of rural fields

in the colours of grasses
for modern walls,
that reminds us
of how hard things were.

This figure stoops
because the plight of all women
through time
has always been
on her shoulders.

These are strong arms
that have held
a child's love
and quietly gathered the grain
for the bread of loved ones
for a thousand years.

There is a pleasure
in the details
of their simple things
that the painter knows.
Of implements, crude blades
and warm wood
simply made,
worn by work,
a beauty in the honest utility
in the hands of generations
of mothers of the earth.

940. Don't worry about creativity,
worry about authenticity.

Reading

I will not read today.
My mind is tired
of too many things.
It is tired of the thoughts
of others.
It needs peace
in thoughts
of its own.

I will look on nature
or spend time
in empty rooms.
I would walk
if I could
across the vast
paddocks of my childhood
at the pace of thought.
To be welcomed home
in the dimming
light of evening
to the aroma
of dinner cooking.

But now I will rest
in the poetry
of silence,
in the silence of my dreams.

ଔ

> **663. "Walking in and out of rooms,**
> that's my cup of tea…."
> - *John Cooper-Clarke*

Sundays

A green-flecked
cast-iron Lux stove
was the center
of her home.
In the warm dark kitchen
of linoleum
it burnt the wood
and scattered orange light
from the fire box,
always open and
a kettle on the boil.

Up the yard
with the grey dirt,
my grandfather's saw
on Sundays screamed
a slow cut that whined through,
revealing the blood colours
within already dead hard trees.

And we kids had to
keep away
because the flat belt
was dangerous.
A ribbon of leather
that snaked from the shed,
through the wall,
whipping toward the saw blade
with the thump, thump
from a green iron flywheel motor.

Now stacked inside,
the firewood
beside my uncle's makeshift bedroom.
A converted, sloping veranda.
As you came in
you could make out,
by the dim laundry window,
bark chips scattered over
the creaks in the floor.

Always on Sunday
we would drive from our town
to hers,
along the Princess Highway to Moe.
I waited for that succulent smell,
as we hurtled from our Chev
the aroma of Nana Wilson's roast
permeated the yard
with deliciousness and bliss.

We ran inside
to the dark paneled walls of the
1920's,
to see her
with a tea-towel-wrapped hand
pull the familiar blacked tray
sizzling from the deep black oven
amid a waft of smoke and steam.

There it was!
A glimpse

of my Sunday desire,
my joy, my heaven.
With bubbling rivulets
draining down the glistening sides
from an off-white salty crust
over angle-cut potatoes
golden with black
like coals from the fire,
she ladled scalding fat.

Please!, please!, please!
I hoped for a crusty bit
like weathered old bark
and oodles of potatoes
that I would hold on my tongue
for longer than necessary
to extend the pleasures
of the palate.

After, when the adults talked,
I would lie on my back
on the grass of the backyard,
squint at the blue summer sky
and revel in my inward pleasure.
A perfect Sunday again!
Perhaps at Trafalgar
we could get chips?

Proust

We live in opposite times
to the time of slow poetry
where things were sharper
in our eyes,
and Proust gazed
at one flower
for an hour
until his friend returned.

And he knew he was
always dying
and had to savor
the small things
to release
the cascade
of sublime memories
that rolled over
the sweet tastes
of his mind.

CR

> **1889. I have no intention
> of remembering** my poems to recite.
> That is the freedom of having no speech.

Absence

The quality of absence
will fill the space
of lost times
and the tragedies
of before.
It will not appease
the places of darkness
and death.
It will not revive
the faded images
of fathers and mothers,
ancestors, to you,
bolt upright
for the lenses
of required stillness.

Emulsions bleach
when they are gone
or they turn sepia
in the grave
of time.
And we, who remain,
for now,
will go the same way,
not living beyond
fragile memories
in the few,
as we too
succumb to the quality
of absence.

Silence Found Me

Silence found me
in the thoughts
of my solitude,
in the wild places
of the mind
and the land
without the noise
of the tropes of men,
spun through the lights
of machines and glass.

It whispered to me
across the vastness
of the sky and the seas,
saying, be still
in your time,
note the rhythms
in the long seasons
of your life
and you will not be lonely
with me.

Solitude Lost

We have lost
the solitude
of once long days.
We can no longer
sit alone
in rooms
with nothing to do.
We can no longer walk the land
with no purpose
other than to be.
All must be instrumental
to our amusement.
We must not face
the void of boredom alone.
We must have intent
in every corner
of our lives.
For if we embrace solitude
our thoughts will come
like banshees in the night
and deflect us
into our uncertainties
and we will fear the madness
we will see.

Beethoven's Window

Today is a good day
for as I arose
I thought
of Beethoven's window,
from the night before.
As he composed,
to keep time
he struck his stick
on the floor.
He looked at a wall
with no window
to see
and although
only rented
had one knocked through.
As a musician
Beethoven definitely knew
the importance
of windows
to assist
his composing muse.

The Railway

'Listen here,'
the barman said,
'ease up you two,
we don't sell fighten beer,
never have.'

Whereupon Stevo
punched Simmo
in the eye
because of something
Simmo had said
with the lucidity
of the mind
that all beer eschews.

It was about his mother
over there,
having fillay minyon
and a well-earned beer.
With her back to the raffle,
hoeing into the chips,
she was oblivious
of the mêlée to be.

No one thought it
would go so far,
but McGillacutty
was also sitting at the bar.
And true to his heritage
and fired by his genes,
he laid in too,
for all it was worth.

After all,
his reputation
was at stake!
and nobody says that
about the bloody church!!!

With the ruckus,
the spilling of beers,
and the upsetting
of tables and chairs
the others,
by necessity,
got involved in the blue.
And pretty soon
it was on
for one and all,
with the bloody audacity
of the bloody cops
bursting through
'our bloody door'
as the punches flew.

It goes without saying
if you're up for a cultured time
go up to Castlemaine
where the locals
are... so, so refined.
And there's plenty of arty stuff
with painters and writers
and poets galore,
in cafes brooding
looking at the floor,

or talking to excess
with a cappuccino
as their muse,
with just a touch
of... must have...
their bio-degradable
fugues
of slow jazz
from behind the bar.

But advice to the real men,
the tradies true blue,
if you are in the real world
and not the bloody dreaming
of the arty bloody few,
have a beer at the bar
of practical men
who defend their mothers,
no if or buts,
right to end,
despite the batons of police,
and no fighting beer,
no pretense
to look cool,
but just to hang out
and be bloody good friends,
to the abso-bloody-lutely
bloody end.

Shadows

1. In the shadows of words
   lies the truth of the lost.
   In the shadows of words
   lie the secrets of our souls.

2. If we ignore the shadows of the words
   we are deaf to what is said.

3. I reveled in the shadows of words.
   Down, down into the abyss
   of a soul,
   laid bare on pages
   translucent to the eyes,
   lies the truth of a poet's thought,
   sublime.

༺ཙ༻

Coleridge's Door
for the protocols of life
and those that interrupt

Coleridge's door haunts me
as I lie without a pen;
they come to me
on Wordsworth's couch,
from that inner voice,
his inward eye.
Associations lost
to a knock,
go out the door,
again.

What Exists?

What exists before he paints?
Thoughts of the time before
he was here?
Thoughts of things
he will never know?
Thoughts of things
to be revealed
to his wandering mind?

He stares at this blank linen
in his quiet space.
There is no sound
but still it will whisper,
someday.

A point to start,
a figure, a form,
an idea not in words.
A stroke of the brush, there!
As he passes, perhaps
casually, on the way
to uncertain things
or suspicious actions
in forceful ways
that betray.

Or, as he stands before it
with defiant authority,
willing to no avail.

Or from his bed in the moonlight
as it plays in his dreams,
waiting for that feeling
of certainty that strikes
gently, from within.
His existential bliss,
to be confirmed by intuition,
not pushed by reason
or a logic of design.
But a fleeting affirmation of his being
to make a move, a gesture
with authenticity.
To use his body and his mind,
there!
Now!
A first note
in a song of paint
he will sing
from a time
revealed
before
he was here.

༄

1885. Poetry is more than words can say.

Poetics and Poetism

What use are poets?
What use are the words
they read?
Do not they confound
the rational,
the pragmatic,
the realists among us?
We, with our feet
on the ground.

Are they not tricksters
and liars,
as Plato said,
and should be
run out of town?
Hiding in the bushes
of hyperbole and hibiscus,
deluding themselves
that they are smarter
than they are?
We are?

With innuendo, rhyme
and metaphor,
what for? Metaphor?
You may ask,
of this obscurantism of fools,
are they not thieves
on the highways
of normality?
Emptying the pockets
of innocence
from our young?

I put to you
that they are dangerous
to all of us
in the real world.
They are scoundrels
who do not work
and we should not trust them,
or dole them out
social sustenance,
for their words of swords
severing sanity
and sensibility
from the world.

They are the bikers
in colors disheveled,
of dubious sophistications,
riding into the towns
of our consciousness
on their loud steeds
of hardly-discernables.

They are the vain
cultural thinkers
who don't shave,
looking at themselves
in the mirror of Narcissus.
Preening themselves
for their next
self-indulgent performance.

And I, for one,
will not enter

into their abuse
of the common vernacular.
I will not condone
the illicit mixing of memes
for diluting
the purity of my common language.
I will not join them,
in pretensions, in the caf de pre-tonse
or be tricked into a black beret
to sprout my prejudices
on their stage of histrionics
exposing their miserable
angst-ridden
view of life.

But, then again,
perhaps they know
more than Plato?
Perhaps they are privy
to truths beyond
our ordinary concerns?
Or can speak of them
in few words, but succinctly?
Perhaps they speak plainly
and are feared by sophists
and charlatans.
Perhaps they are dismissed
by the ignorant and slain
by conquering armies
because they dare to think
and do so with effect on others?
And perhaps they die penniless
because their words
are priceless
to our souls.

I DO NOT REASON
WHY A LINE
THAT APPEARS
BENEATH MY HAND
IS SO SUBLIME
I DO NOT KNOW
FROM WHERE IT CAME
I DO NOT KNOW WHERE
IT IS GOING
OR WHEN IT WILL END
BUT STILL I MOVE
AND THIS SPACE WITH NO REASO
IN WORDS OR DESIGN
JUST WITH FAITH
THAT IT IS RIGHT
TO CONTINUE
ALONG THIS PATH IN TIME
AGAINST MY FEARS
THAT I MAY BE WRONG
IN FAITH I TRAVEL
FOR I HAVE LEARNT
DOWN MANY YEARS
THAT A LINE IS A SONG
THAT SHOULD HAVE NO FEAR

In the Air

Like music and dance,
art happens in the air.
A halfway trans-action
forming mind through body
not for all to sense,
not for all to see.
Between the stone
and Henry Moore,
between the paint
and thinking eyes.
Long stillness and intuition,
the body and the canvas,
the pen and the page.
Like Merwin's pencil
with words crouching
in the graphite darkness,
waiting to form on the outside.

Between intention and action,
between the lens and the land,
between beauty and reason,
between body and matter
there is a unity.
They are one and the same.
In the space between
the mind and the travelling line,
a thought formed in action.
In the space between
the watched and the watcher,
without effort to meet halfway,
in the air they will not sense,
will not think or see.

The Poet

In the shadow of his hand
the pen moves deftly,
gliding into the light of thought,
and moves the darkness
from his soul.

ଊ

> **1856. I listen to write.**

ଊ

The Painter

The painter lives amongst
ordinary things
and hones a craft
quietly through the days
of doubts,
in rooms of despair,
to discover fleetingly
the jewels of life,
on canvas
laid bare.

The Sculptor
for Trefor Prest

He has scant use
for words.
He speaks to the world
through hands that know
the pleasures of machines,
the feel of metals, wood,
and metaphors.
From a time where
we were one
with silken metals formed
in gold.

Writhe levers
act with questions
and lead the mind
to a sculptor's delight
in our expectations
of purpose,
of reasons to function
in breasts and bones,
transformed,
our eyes moving
from biology to mechanism
and back again.

Handles invite movement
of our curiosities
to drive a complexity
of gearings that lead us
to doubt our pragmatism,
to despair.

Canvas, diving helmets and wings,
exquisitely formed metaphors
morphing into nautical shapes
lost at sea.
Delicate insects
of wires, brass, and wood
left or discovered
between the peasant
spreading the seeds
and the stories in things,
in the language
of memories,
without words.

સર

1859. I look to write.

Thoughts Have Wings

Thoughts have wings
like trapped birds.
For a while
they fly into
the rooms of our thinking.

Beyond grasping,
for a while,
desperately seeking,
sometimes in panic,
for freedom,
a way out perhaps.
Wings beating,
losing feathers,
breaking our sacred ornaments
of the mind.

They might frighten us
as strange intruders do,
while we wave arms of reason
or faith,
from the floor
of our certainties
as we set conceptual traps
to no avail.

Sometimes in vagueness
when I enter a room,
I find a black crow sitting
with one ancient eye
fixed on me.

As I circle in ignorance
there is a fear
from a hundred nights
in me.
Deep from history
it watches,
as if to say,
'try and take hold,
if you dare,
again.'

Sometimes in dreams
I enter by accident, perhaps,
these dark rooms
and there is light
and a thousand nightingales
suspended, still,
for my examination,
for weighing
one against the other.

Sometimes the little finches
fly out as quickly
as I step in.
They are lost to eternity,
to the wild,
from which they came.
Or to find the rooms of others
and torment them.
If they see them there,
if they bother
to enter.

But my pleasure is ecstasy
when in casual wanderings
I pass by a window or door
to enter,
and find standing
still,
with a clarity perfect,
in the alertness of the sun
that bird of paradise
has come.
One thought glowing
in a room.

Having flown
the great distances of mind,
weathered the storms of despairs,
over the synaptic mountains
of doubts,
along the rills of reason,
down to the valley of rooms.

Arriving,
clear and succinct,
in a poetry of insight,
the poetry of light
that settles,
between the walls
of wisdoms grasped,
in the rooms of my bliss.

Drawing 2

I find
I do not reason
why a line
that appears slowly
beneath my hand
is good.
I do not know
where it came from
and I will not know
where it will go,
or where it will end.
But still,
the hand moves
and leaves this trace
on this page
with no reason or picture
quietly hiding in my mind.
In faith and pleasure
it travels blind
along this foreign path
against the doubts
but with my knowing
there is a song
in every line.

☙

> **1860. I write to think.**

Hands

I remember
my hands
in a room
on Rue de Charenton.
Looking at them
I thought
they were always old.

They ached
in a new way,
unknown to me
or them.
I sensed old habits,
old assumptions
denied,
from somewhere
foreign to this place,
foreign to small rooms.

Perhaps we felt
for things lost,
to cafes and transit lounges,
to Heidegger and croissants.
Now, unbalanced,
it was a longing,
too late,
for the feel of metal
or wood,
of familiar tools
with stories,
on benches, in sheds.

Although adept
at turning pages
with thoughts
in the sun
and making notes
in the Jardin des Plantes,
there was more.

A long-forgotten craving,
for the pleasures of new thoughts
in the feeling of things evolving,
with the bliss of textures
through these hands,
stirred
like a thirst
in my throat
with no hope of water,
in these small rooms.

⁂

> **2084. Writing poetry is a distillation**
> into the self, while in the same action forming the
> new self.

Excuse Me, Monsieur

After a few days
of her hospitality,
in desperation,
she said she knew rock stars
in London.
As if it would goad me
into her bed.

In a hurry, before patients' talks,
she would make
lukewarm coffee
from the hot tap,
dip in a cold croissant, chew.
And, as always, smoked.

At those times,
it was organised.
I had to be out!
I would wander the streets of Paris
until a preordained time.
I didn't mind.

We went on excursions
to show an Australian
what he didn't know.
I didn't apologise,
I didn't even mind.

One evening
I found myself with her
in a basement exhibition.
A show of provincial art,
not good,

but the drinks were free.

'Excuse me, monsieur!'
In a crowded vault,
with an all-white suit
and broad-rimmed hat
to match,
and white goatee,
he smiled,
and was frail.

Although I tried to avoid
this curious man,
although I wanted to talk,
again and again,
we stepped around each other
three times an evening.
Three,
'excuse me, monsieur!'

Who was that old man in white?
I questioned
when I was let in.
That was Miro!
Agitated,
'don't you know anything?'

Later, I thought
perhaps we could have talked
about many things.
But, unlike her,
I was not frustrated,
culturally exasperated.
I didn't mind,
so I let him in.

Harley Triumph
for Phil and Jules

I have ridden
amongst the colours
of the tribes of men.
On the highways
to our oblivion
across the lands
of our souls.

With machines
beneath us
breathing a fire within
their heavy throb
open to gauntlet hands
on the throttles of power
accelerating us
into the ecstasy
of pulling away.
Pulling away
from the blight
of suburban despair
and the descent
into the boredom of us all
that few understand.

On the black blurred
bluestone and concrete ribbons
of the freeway
to our lives,
beneath fat wheels,
there is escape

into the bliss of metal machines,
denim, and a lust
for a life to be lived.

I have ridden
to the music
of the pipes blued hard
by combustion's flames,
fusing the history
of warrior men,
chromed loud
and deep
onto the roads
of their being.

ଙ

> **1372. I like men who know
> the poetry of machines.**

Herbert the Exaggerator

He is not faster than a speeding bullet,
not as powerful as a locomotive,
he is unable to leap tall buildings
in a single bound
like he says.
He is in no way able to be in the sky
because of his vertigo.
'Look, it isn't a bird! Look, it isn't a plane!!'
He has no powers beyond mortal men,
he can't change the course of mighty rivers,
he can't bend steel in his bare hands.
It's not Herbert from a distant planet at all,
from whence he came to fight
for peace, justice and the American way!!!
He is just from around the corner.

He is not disguised as Herbert,
HE IS HERBERT!!
And has too much to say of himself
and wears underpants over his jeans,
much to the annoyance of his mother.

CR

> **1967. I didn't realise** how much I enjoyed
> being read poetry in primary school
> and without any inkling that,
> from this enjoyment, I could write poetry;
> only poets did that.

First Line Dilemma
in response to an ABC R.N. program

It was a dark and stormy night.
The night was dark and stormy.
The night was dark and the weather was bad.
The night was black and the weather was bad.
The night was sort of dark
and the weather was not good.
It was night,
and the weather was dark and stormy.
In the night-time there was a black storm.
In the night-time there was a storm
and it was dark.
In the night-time it was really dark
and really stormy.
At night there was a storm, and a black dog.
The black dog howled at the night
because it was stormy.
The black dog howled at the moon
but he couldn't see it because of the storm.
The dog was black and stormy.
In the night there was a dark dog called stormy.
In the storm the black dog got wet in the dark.
He found a black dog on a stormy night
and it was wet.
There was a black dog that found a man
on a dark and stormy night.
On that dark night of a storm,
a black wet dog called Stormy bit the man.
The black dog and the dark man
had nothing to do with the stormy night.
And so on and on
into the dark and stormy night
with a black, wet dog.

If Apples fell Sideways

If apples fell sideways
where would Newton be?
He would be walking by,
not under his tree.

If apples fell sideways
what would he do?
Would it be difficult for him
to put on his shoes?

And when dropped,
would his quill
go to the wall?
Would we have to change
the concept
'to fall'?

Would he concede
that pigs could fly
as he looked out
his window
as a pig went by?

Would he be prompted
to start again,
page after page
cursing his pen?

Would his room be a mess
to grapple in vain,
as chairs went out
his window again?

Would gravity be universal
or just where he stood?
Would patrons be puzzled
on a stool at the bar
as sideways he slid?

Would we be beside ourselves
when he was near?
And swear to never
take to drink again!
Would we dispute
philosophia
as a farce not fit
for the likes of sober men?

I suspect
he would give up his *Principia*
and mathematics too.
That light was particles
would come to an end.
He would give up writing as well
as his ink went sideways
as it left his pen.

The direction of an apple
would have changed a man's life.
Not to mention
giving the pips
as he fell from grace,
not like an apple,
to his long suffering wife.

Certainties

Some thoughts
come to me
clothed in the night
of my darkness.

They are shadows
behind curtains
not venturing
into reason's light.
Like the flight
of frightened birds
they escape
as I feel the pressure
of fleeing wings,
in the night
of my darkness.
They are lost
to the banalities
of my certainties.

ଔ

---

673. No one tells you to do art or write poetry, it is a choice, and it's a choice I wouldn't recommend for most people who need security.

Her Truth
for A.L.

Every time
she came into
the reason of light
her shadows extended
into the eerie madness
where she remained,
alone,
in those endured days.

And the things around
needed to be explained,
in a clarity lost to her
that crystallised her nights
into the old creatures
of her fears.

But she knew,
in her multiple worlds,
she would never be far
from the combustion
of her internal flame.
Never far
from the abstract darkness,
the long knives
of shadows from the moon
that burnt through her soul
when she touched
her sadness within.

For a Girl

I don't know you,
but great artists
and philosophers do.
You are old to them.
Your anguish and desperation
is real to their souls.

You have been with them
on the mountains of beauty.
You have been
with all your women before you,
and they know your pain.

You are their hope.
They can no longer
fulfill their dreams.
Your dreams in hopelessness
are theirs.
They had the same sadness
before you were born.
They had the same suffering
before you were born.
Only you remain to suffer
because you are human.

They would say,
if you listen
to the whispers
in your soul,
it is hard
but keep living,
so our pain is not wasted.

Keep living
so our babies
are still in our hearts
and yours.

You are not alone
as you think you are.
We are here
and you
are all our dreams.

₢₨

2012. As Sartre's Existence precedes Essence, the action of the pen or the keyboard precedes the meaning of the text or drawing.

Hat

reflection from the loved hills of Boolarra

With a twinkle in his eyes,
he said 'that used to be
my Sunday-go-to-meeting hat,
now look at it!'

We were up in the paddock at the time,
baling done, grey Fergy running,
pipe refilling,
ready to head home.

The stubble was golden
and his remarks wry
as we paused in the still, hot air
high on that hill above home.

As always, Jack's hats started out
new and smart
as he walked toward the car
on those Sundays,
heading into town,
a few hours without work
and a new hat!

There was a separate hat
for the paddocks.
On the kitchen table
resting, it too, once had privilege
and went to town.

But now
with a few holes worn through,
or perhaps from barbed wire,
its only company the cat
and the ticking of the lounge room clock.

For a long time now,
a black patina of work
had flattened the rabbit's fine fur,
from a few seasons of sweat, perhaps.
Although, I can't remember a time
when it was not like that,
not his hat.
Weathered, like it had always been
up the paddocks,
in the yards,
with Jack.

Always a non-descript shape,
but keeping out most of the rain,
always ready to be thrown to the ground
because a bloody stupid mongrel cow
won't go through a bloody gate.

Like a man's shoes or boots,
a man's hat indicates the man.
And Jack's hat had worked hard,
with dignity, without pretention,
with a bit of humor
and, although not said,
was loved,
as was the man.

I Could Not Speak to Her

I could not speak to her.
Did I know her?
In my fears
she was there.
In some women I knew
she would appear
naked,
fighting, screaming
in the distance,
on the ridge
in the wild bush,
amongst the boulders
of my nightmares.
Thrashing down the gullies,
wild eyes spitting.
Feral creature
against all reason.
Protesting fury
against all men,
against all women,
from a failed father within.

CR

> **1280. Sometimes I am lost**
> in the long shadows of thought.

God for Certainty

He revels in the comfort
of his certainties,
in that sanctuary
of zealots
that fear the madness
of the other.

He is certain his God
is with him
as he draws the blade
deep across the throat
of an infidel kneeling,
bleeding to his command.

He revels in the comfort
of his certainties
behind the zephyr
of magnetic waves
where every building,
every rock, even humanity
is pixilated,
abstracted to a game,
digitized into a dream,
in a grand theft auto
of adolescent impotence
that smears the limbs of children
across bonnets and sand,
in the certainty
that God is with him,
and the certainty that
the other is mad.

From Schubert

From Schubert,
there is a sadness
in the hands
of a musician
that rises
from both
their souls.

Of slow sounds
as soft hammers
under fingers,
caresses metal strings
through the humanity
of us all.

ଔ

Listen

I heard a nun say
'we must listen
with ears of the heart'
and 'violence comes
from those not heard',
and wondered
how I knew these words.

Singing in Darkness

Every soul is a universe
confined in a room of dreams
singing in the darkness of reason
a voice at the beginnings of being.

ଓ

> **1311. Poetry purely for the joy of sound,**
> rhythm and tongue, with an underlying hint of sense.

ଓ

The Architect

She watched
the unnoticed things
to learn from the alignments
of her efforts
with the transient
wind, the rain, the sun,
the flow of people,
the words in rooms,
and with the passing of the clouds
these accidents of her architecture
were her new mysteries
to be explained.

The Thickness of Walls

Walls are thicker in the dark,
I have felt them grow
metres out into the night,
from weatherboards
and stone.
Beyond the garden,
organised,
to the wild eucalyptus stands
at the border of my world,
at the border of my eyes.

Some doors are heavy
when opened to the moon.
The windows blacken
when often closed,
upsetting my notion of time.
Some walls reflect
a word not spoken
in an empty room.
Beyond their surfaces
a whisper stills,
then fades across the land.

1350. I collect words, things
and situations of alignments.

All Buildings

Like nature
all buildings
have secrets.
Beautiful secrets
that reveal themselves
to the unhurried mind
in the right place
at the right time.

A shaft of light
unintended,
a shadow not there.

From the lowly shed
to the temple of Sagrada Familia,
surprising even their makers,
passing secrets appear
in still moments
of metal, mortar, glass and stone,
often unimportant,
but noticed
by the unhurried mind.

ଔ

> **1183. All my life** I have wandered
> with pleasure through words.

When we Build in Stone

When we build in stone
it is a different thing
to building in brick,
the rational brick
from a factory line of clay
whose mathematics is known,
geometry the same,
engineered for prediction,
enabling the craftsman layer
and others as well
to see a wall
in the future
of regular grids and lines
all the same,
decisions relegated,
labor in vain
bricks uniform repeating
again and again
by the string
and the level
between the red and the white,
verticals and horizontals
in perfect perspective receding,
yielding
to the drawing,
to the specifications clear,
to the pragmatic mind,
to the bureaucracy of forms
that they hold so dear.

But when we build in stone
we sing slow songs
with the elements
of the field
and coming to the light
from a million years,
the poetry of stone unearthed
is a different thing,
the future placement unknown,
the final patterns not clear.
Each stone a universe
for decisions
placed by intuition
by the mason's hand
from shapes remembered
until the last one is laid
in the sureness of artistry,

a dance with nature begins
in solidity and light
of contours and subtle hues,
a landscape for contemplations,
a wall for the moon
stretching through the night,
a painting for the garden
in the drifting afternoon.
A painting done in stone,
that is a different thing.

Boollara Farm 2, 1956

When there,
before I saw I was,
I knew what was important
in those long days
of a child's mind,
in the valleys,
down at the creek.

Sounds and the dark
under the split logs
that made the grey warm bridge,
with bolts,
across the paddock
to the always empty road.

Near the milking shed,
still with it's shush, shush, shush,
back up the high crown track
away from the tree-fern gully
always watching me sing.

Centrifugal force was learnt
from the swinging of one straight arm
with a billy of milk
for the house
and warm bread
wrapped in white tissue.

I did not spill the milk,
knowing what was important
in those Gippsland hills,
for my child's mind
before I barely knew I was.

Rock, Hand, Rain and Air

I have a thought
for my hand.
To have it as a deep imprint
in flat rock
on my land,
so when it rains
the hand fills with water,
and when the sun shines
in the afternoon
the hand is projected
at a certain time,
onto a large rock.
And if there is a breeze,
the water in my hand will ripple
and my hand on the rock
will wave to you.

ଔ

1831. Stone poems for the land.
Poetry on the rocks.

Broken Things

There is a truth
in the broken things
of the world.
We can pass them over
or see a history
in the rage, in passions throwing,
spinning across space
of things lost
or betrayed
from where things were,
in unsung agreements,
to where things are now,
between lovers, family or friends.

Broken things
talk, perhaps, in fractures
once succinct,
along lines of neglect
not repaired by time.

A knife shatters in a drawer
as tensions in a family
no longer can be sustained.

A coffee pot explodes
onto a ceiling, across a room
as husband and wife
slip deeper into despair,
as a deep brown dripping down walls
stains a not-forgotten affair.

A cup descends to floor
to shatter into puzzles
of the soul,
broken pieces of shame,
the truth in a silence profound,
never to be repaired,
never to be resolved,
lost but not found
in the broken things
of the world.

ख

982. Poets speak quietly
but carry a bigger stick.

Legacies

I have drawn
three spikes
of no particular relevance.
Made,
an object to be explained.
I have placed
a mirror in the air,
measured reflections
after the rain.
Watched a burning line
on the land,
an anamorphic shadow,
unselbstandigkiet
across the sand.

I have said a word
to form a cube
and travel up the stairs.
I have drawn an image
of a chair
again and again.
A category of intellect,
a blueprint for the mind.
With the pleasure of conscious thought,
an object to be explained.
These are the objects
I leave behind, and
they are the shadows
in your mind.

Before

There is that place
of quiet wanderings
over the fields
of the mind.

A space of connections
procured
from the darkness
of the sublime.

The place before the words ap-
pear,
before the pen crosses the page,
before the gesture drawn,
before the action of the brush,
before the note not played.

A place I am meant to be
for the poetry
of the brush
without the oil.
The poetry of words
not on the page,
the silent poetry
of thoughts not yet known,
before the movement of the pen
or the clicking of black keys,
the poetry
of my sanity.

Headstone of a Rationalist

I have assessed
the empirical adequacy
of my existence
and concluded
I am not here
or anywhere else.

༄

He Wanted to be Heard

He wanted to be heard,
so he climbed a tree
and did a tweet.

༄

Big-noting Myself

I heard a knock
at my door.
It was Coleridge,
and I lost it!

Writers

Flann O'Brien
and Wittgenstein
together in a room.
Wittgenstein has a thought,
O'Brien only four,
two beginnings
and two endings
for Wittgenstein's ladder
against the wall.
Will they
work together
or be prisoners
of their metaphors?

ଔ

Poets

I notice male poets don't
shave.
And they often wear black
hats.
Do they see themselves
as the bad guys
in spaghetti western literature?

The Logic of Bathing

In his ritual of showering
four things aligned.
The rationality of a father,
the prudery of a grandmother,
a childhood spent
on tank water,
and the Jesuits
(via an unknown grandfather).

There was a procedure
always adhered to.
Firstly for the tank
and the father.
He would not turn on the water
immediately.
Rather, he would,
using liquid soap
apply to his hair, face, arms, trunk and
legs
by the expressed logical instructions
from his father
to always wash a car from the roof down.

Standing in a cold cubicle
(for the Jesuits)
he would then apply soap
to his nether regions
(without looking)
which was a conscious deference
to his grandmother,
but do so VIGOROUSLY,
in deference to his father.

For the tank,
he would not put the hot
on full blast,
but rather just a fraction, adding cold,
then quickly move under
the showerhead and scrub everywhere
for thirty seconds (father and tank)
with a coarse brush,
(without looking at nether regions)
as deference to a Jesuit ancestry,
which is a celibate contradiction.

In keeping with his theme
he would always prefer
cardboard-stiff towels
to dry (Jesuits)
only feeling for nether regions
(grandmother and Jesuits)
and not looking.

He found peace in this ritual
that always cleansed his body and soul
and wondered (not in the shower)
if this logic had other applications
(father, tank, grandmother and Jesuits).

☙

> **780. Now in my sixties,**
> I realize how many thoughts I may have lost
> by getting up early.

Old Hands
in memory of George Duffel

I look at my hands
now, with pleasure
in the tiredness of my skin,
the craggy landscape of years.
Raised veins move
as I flex my fingers
slowly, in thoughts
of the hands I wanted
to have,
that I loved,
at times lost.

From a child
I was in awe of the hands
of farmers,
of my uncles,
they were the hands
of stories,
of the yards,
the milking sheds
and the bush.

'One day'
I will have hands like them.
Hands that knew work,
hands that threw the firewood
from the saw
in old bush sheds.

Hands that fenced
and quietly dug holes
for years in the rain
over lonely hills.
Hands that made things
as I have done
with pleasures worn.

Every furrow line,
chipped nail
that wrapped around a mug
as they unfurled
red checked gingham
from a basket
up the paddock
was testament to a life
hard won,
through hands
that learnt the wisdom
of the earth.

ଔ

> **2133. When I write poetry**
> I aim to have my feet firmly on the ground,
> not up in the wistful clouds.

Night Shooting

I remember those nights
when I walked with Jack
out across the dew-wet grass
into the blackness, through the wires
held open, taught by foot and hand,
in an etiquette of the paddock
that city people didn't know.

I had pestered him to go.
'Oh well! I suppose
we better go round the traps,'
so we went with an old 22
resting on his left arm, pointing to the ground
while I held the bullets
in my pockets.

Those nights were precious
as I drew in the moist cool air
across my tongue to taste it
and it mingled with the sweet smell of cow
dung
that went in and out of my young nostrils
to the sound of swishing
and the dull thud of our gumboots
through the sodden grass underfoot.

I hoped there weren't bunnies in the traps
but I kept this to myself,
and hoped for a shot
of that old 22
worn smooth with dark greasy wood
from years on this place.

Once we forgot the spotlight
that strafed the contours
of quiet hiding hills
and would send back
the eyes of body-less cows
or the red glint of a rabbit's eye
keeping still on the edge of the bracken.
But Jack let me fire a few rounds
that crack-echoed around the unseen hills
and ricochet in my thoughts still.

I remember kneeling
in that bracken,
Jack's black boot pressing down
on the flat spring to release dead rabbits
with one still eye staring up at me
and the wet fur of their feet,
still warm,
held tight in my small hand
as we trooped back
to the house's distant kerosene glow.

I remember pragmatisms
mixed with morality as I watched,
from the breeze-way of the milking shed,
as Jack skinned and gutted them
with hardly a thought
of their previous quickening.

I remember the thoughts
of contradictions splitting me
and the smile on my grandmother's face

as she relished our pending roast.

It seems nature has decreed
that its creatures tear each other apart
and we are only left with the horror
of memories slain by consciousness.

༄

---

795. What to write, what to do?
When I write I begin not with a plan
but a powerful impression or feeling that has come
into my body/mind. It may have been triggered
by words I overheard or a memory of things past.
But the words start, particularly in poetry,
with a fixation, perhaps, on a single line of words
that is the first line. It then evolves from there with
no idea what is coming next. The first line triggers
the next line and so on, just through the physical
action of writing, similar to the progression
in painting or making things.
Thoughts need physical action to proceed.

Rage
for Kerryn

I feel rage for her.
How assumptions
and codified ideas
of how life should proceed
robbed a diligent girl,
for a while,
of a passion
for discovering colours
in the city
on the way home.
She was excited
over new pencils.

But there was no malice
in their denial, just hope
that she would use her brain
because she had a curse,
she was good at everything.
But still the magic of paper,
of the useless marks beneath her hand,
the lines of not knowing
calls her over her years.
Beauty is in her heart,
by the afternoon sun
across a table
in a dining room.
There is hope.
She has begun again.

You Read to Me

You read to me
the wise words
of the fallen.
You read to me
the wisdom
of the dead.

You read to me
the sorrows of
the poets.
You read to me
the words
of the painters
lost in the light
'till their end.

You read to me
the sounds
of their anguish,
how the brush
was replaced
by the pen.

You read to me
the plight of Reason.
You read to me
fear of the faithful
down on their knees
in hell.

When will these pages end?
When will the words
be taken for stories
and submit to the flames
of the zealots of certainty
in the name of God.
When will you
read to me again?

༄

1163. In poetry and writing
the first line produces the next and I never know
what the next line will be until I complete it.
It is the same in painting or drawing; the first mark
begets the following mark and so on.
It is the same with concepts for me;
the first concept begets the following and so on.
An orange leads to a planet that leads to the garden
of my childhood that leads to the importance of
dreams, and so on, for a lifetime.

Not There

It's too late for ideas,
like geometry
the words are not true,
they are simply advantageous
shadows cast from
our thoughts.
In our desperate race
to take hold,
to grasp,
we see
a light
not there.

ೞ

> **1131. I write poetry** in the same mental state from which I paint.

ೞ

Need

I feel I need a lonely sound.
A cello that takes me
to a place for my soul
to rest
amongst the sounds
of dreams.

Equation

James Joyce twice plus
Picasso to the power
of Duchamp
by Husserl bracketed
divided by Wittgenstein weeping
slowly to Mozart's
Piano Concerto No. 21.

ଊ

Houses without Pianos

Houses without pianos
rooms without soul
doors without hope
of nowhere to go
through windows
with no light
on tables bare
of kind words
in the afternoon sun
there is no one,
no one
in these walls
without music,
in these walls
of despair.

Anglesea
for Kerryn

From time to time
she took me back
along the twisturning
Ocean Road
only to the edge
of her lost home
on the coast cliffs
of her childhood.

Named from the time
of far-away tribes
her town was
the sea of the Angles
on an antipodean shore
of lost parents
from better days.

Now, she does not
take me to her home
on the hill
just up there.
It is too much
to see her loss.

From time to time
to overlay memories
with the present
can be a sad thing,
so we travel on

past happy times
as she points out
the beach, the river
of dreams with her brothers
in canoes.

Life now is not the same
in hired houses
with her new family
on the coast
of regrets
born of pragmatisms
that ignored a child's heart.
Although the sound
of the waves
brings her back
to warm securities
as we fall asleep.

※

1767. Writing poetry requires empathy.

Hills

I realise I prefer hills
than large flat lands.
I have known
and walked or worked
in the heat,
along channels,
along dusty roads of silence
save for gravel crackling
under my boots.
Slow to the horizon
of boredom,
of longing
for a hill of green,
a shallow dip to a creek
not there.
I realise I prefer hills
than the flat lands
of hot dry despairs.

☙

> **943. Walking has the pace of thought,**
> particularly if it has no purpose.

Blackness

I love the blackness
caused by the rain
in the night,
on the stones,
in the streets
of cold wanderings.

I am content
with every step,
with heavy coat,
sodden boots,
in the midst
of pleasures,
of the mind
working for the soul.

Words come
in the slow stream
of reflections,
out of the blackness
caused by rain.

༄

2049. Poetry is a compression of complex ideas and feelings into simpler words.

Leon 4 one 5

for Leon Szepetko, a friend,
who taught me things

When I remember him
I think of Bertrand Russell's socks.
I remember his giggling
and mischievous eyes,
revealing to me
from the dank darkness
of a Dorrit Street terrace
smelling of paint,
Marlborough cigarettes,
coffee, and always, the red wine,
the intimate details of great men.
Who they actually slept with,
what they liked to do in those beds,
was a glee to him.

Manically, I realise now,
he painted and wrote poetry.
He was into Jung
before it was hippy cute.
He constructed great diagrams
with explicit meanings
of unconscious stories
from his Russian mind,
a lupine howl
from the winds on the steppes
of his ancestors.

Always nervously smoking,
pacing and changing direction.
Always Frank Sinatra
was spoken about
in sudden hushed tones
and I was often made to sit
and listen for the revelations
from the master.

Although Frank was not so precious
as the mania to draw
and colour-in strange creatures
cavorting amongst snakes-
and-ladders-like diagrams.

The energy in poor circumstances
was to grab what was at hand.
Cook porridge dry with cocoa
in op-shop pots.
Precious LPs became palettes
smeared with paint,
later to hang like trophies
on Fitzroy walls
above Henry's Dickensian shoe shop
at 4 one 5 Brunswick Street.

He would do the rounds,
smoking like a professor
while squinting his eyes
in a 'yes, but –' manner.

Speak home truths
to off-guard friends
and make himself unpopular.
Countering with a knife of precision
all their tearful remonstrations.
And leave to the streets again.

Although he never confronted me.
I suspect
I was a puzzle to be respected.
Ollie was used to him.
A fellow Russian bohemian
acting in Beckett's Godot
with the New Theatre.
In the city,
Jack Charles sleeping on the couch,
he always smiled
and understood his friend.

Frank Mustache,
as he called him,
was there
when he dropped dead
at the end of the kitchen table,
amongst Buddhists,
in some outer suburb.

He said from a dream
he knew he was about to die,
but none listened
until he did.

We speculated
that he knew his fate
from a railways medical
and then went hell-for-leather
into life
before it ended.

Later his friends
had a show of his work,
in Greensborough
or somewhere.
I met established painter friends there.
They said,
pity he died
when he was just getting good.

⊗

> **1405. A good poem introduces me** to a concept
> or feeling succinctly but not completely;
> it leaves me with further puzzles
> on the edge of my grasping,
> giving me further things to think about.

Going Back

I do not go back
to the places
of precious memories.
To the land,
the tracks and roads,
the houses and sheds.
To the bush of the hills,
the country town verandas
of my youth
that dwell in my soul.

The fences I loved
are gone,
with a nausea
when there.
Through the windows
of my fast, modern car
a slow sadness is felt
as I overlay
the scenes of now
with memories clear
from lost years.

Subtle interferences
in my heart
form moiré patterns
with history,
cancelling the good,
reinforcing the loss.
A thinning of memory
through glass appears.

As a foreigner
in my own land
I prefer dreams
to sensible plans
and
I do not want
to be here
again.

༺ཨ༻

> **2175.** If art or poetry is too far abstracted from experience, it's useless.

Before School

Before school,
I said to my mother:
poets have to sleep in
until they get
their first line.
She replied:
I like Wordsworth,
so take a walk!

ଊ

Blind

Sometimes
I see unimportant things
that flow throughout our lives.
They are the shadows of ourselves,
to which we are too often
blind.

ଊ

Clock

We only notice the ticking
when it stops.
Stops, stops, stops…………

Ancestor's Hands

By our ancestors hands
drawing was singing
in the sand

and by their voice
a song was
a drawing in the air.

༄

Omissions

Sometimes he heard
the quiet, soft space
between her words.
They were like the road
when he stopped
to look into the distance.

They were a gap
so small,
on the liminal edge
of his knowing,
but he knew
she said a lot
in these omissions.

Lost

On the green land
without horizons
I was still as I lay
in old rooms,
feeling, sensing it
as it went away
around the hills
of Gippsland,
to Boolarra and beyond,
above the bush.
In my mind I imagined it
as it went through a window
of my dreams,
out to the black highways.
To the smoke-filled valley
of white towers
it is lost
to reason.

Lost to distractions,
in rational rooms
of commission houses,
of solid geometry,
smooth walls of cement sheets
and calculations for frames
milled from the trees,
that hugged the free roads
of my youthful sensibilities.

I do not know
what was lost
but I feel it deeply.
Perhaps it is from
becoming old,
a state of being
in a familiar place,
but lost
amongst familiar things.

Perhaps it is
outside my words
and trying, to no avail,
to get back in?
Perhaps it is an
innocence of the soul
succumbing
to a reasonable world,
but lost,
all the same.

൭

> **307. The limits of words**
> are exemplified in their inability
> to convey the call of the common magpie.

Breathing
for Kerryn, past midnight on her birthday

From our other room
in the quiet of my thoughts
I hear a sound
from elsewhere,
the long slow air
of your breathing
as you sleep.
It is our living,
that I know
is precious.
We are together
in our dreaming,
in your breathing
I breathe,
and
we are as one.

2329. Poetry is about what we felt
before we had words.

Oblivion

The land,
the land is flat
and I am in there,
on there,
of there,
in my way
I am one there.
And the birds of my thoughts
flee to the horizon
of my soul
and call in the nights
of my forever dreams.
To be seen
in the lust of my passions
I leave you now
for my flat lands
of my oblivion.

☙

1154. Perhaps the next poem or painting or photograph I do will hit the nail on the head.

www.ingramcontent.com/pod-product-compliance
Lightning Source LLC
Chambersburg PA
CBHW070618300426
44113CB00010B/1578